Drawn to Scottish Steam

Drawn to Scottish Steam

Bill Rhind Brown & Dugald Cameron OBE

Strathwood

"Drawn To Scottish Steam"

A selection of photographs of the steam railway mainly around Glasgow and Edinburgh by Bill Rhind Brown and Dugald Cameron OBE with an appreciation of railway enthusiasm and some of the personalities of yesteryear by Campbell Cornwell.

We dedicate this book to their memory and especially to John Thomas and in doing so remember the many rewarding friendships and aquaintanceships made over the years all of whom were drawn to steam and the railway.

Page 1: In the early 1930's, passenger trains on the Aberdeen-Edinburgh road were limited to loads of 420 tons up and 480 tons in the down direction for Gresley A1 - A3 Pacifics; double heading was forbidden. To avoid resorting to relief trains, something quite new was required and Gresley designed the unexpected and revolutionary P2 2-8-2 locomotives. The A4s and the V2 had not yet reached the drawing boards. Rumours and speculation were rife among enthusiasts. Understandably, the public too took great interest in railway progress; railways were the nation's main means of transport for passengers and goods. Enthusiasts and the press had a field day when the first of the new class, No 2001, rolled out of the Doncaster plant in May 1934, appropriately named *Cock O The North* in view of the future Aberdeenshire connection. It may be of interest to readers to know that Marie De Guise, mother of Mary Queen of Scots, on a visit to Huntly Castle, coined the nickname 'Cock o the North' for her host, the Marquis, at that time the most powerful noble in Scotland. The sobriquet is still applied to the head of the family. (The late John Brown)

Frontispiece: This was the occasion when Dugald first met Campbell Lawson Kerr, the noted photographer of Scottish railways in the Autumn of 1963 at Polmadie, when they both took a picture of A2/3 60524 *Herringbone* on the lunchtime local to Carlisle from Glasgow Central. (Dugald Cameron OBE)

Left: A new and as yet un-named Peppercorn A1 60161 (*North British*) attacking Cowlairs Bank in great style, in late December 1949, just two weeks into traffic in the then new BR standard blue. (The late John Thomas)

Right: The unique and remarkable transporter wagon used to carry new locomotives to the quayside on curves they may not accept themselves, designed by the late Harold John Cornwell. (Campbell Cornwell Collection)

First published 2005

ISBN 1-905276-00-1

Published by Strathwood Ltd

Introduction

Some Railway Enthusiasts I Have Known

One of the characteristics of a developed and civilised society is that it caters for a wide range of activities, tastes and interests. In addition to the familiar academic disciplines taught in schools and universities, there are numerous other subjects of academic interest and value, some of which have been, the province as much of the amateur as the professional. For a nation like ours with a glorious industrial and engineering heritage, it is not surprising that people not professionally involved in these matters have taken an informed and very special interest in them. While railways in general, and the steam locomotive in particular, are closely followed by many thousands of amateurs in this and other western countries, little has been recorded of those who have contributed most to the subject through their research, writing and photography as well as by their efforts in setting up and running the

numerous amateur societies and commercial publications. I have used the word 'amateur', not in a derogatory sense but in reference to the fact that the vast majority of railway enthusiasts are neither railway employees nor members of a professional railway or engineering institution. Nevertheless, many professional railwaymen and railway engineers share that same fascination with the steam locomotive felt by their amateur brethren and there has been much collaboration between the two. Indeed, the professional Institution of Locomotive Engineers, now part of the Institution of Mechanical Engineers, was an offshoot of the amateur Stephenson Locomotive Society.

The first railway enthusiast I met, and this happened very soon after my birth, was my father, the late Harold John Cornwell. After obtaining his

qualifications in mechanical engineering in Glasgow's Royal College of Science and Technology (RCST), now the University of Strathclyde, he did an apprenticeship with the North British Locomotive (NBL) Company and then moved to Armstrong Whitworth & Company on Tyneside. There he designed a bogie wagon capable of carrying an Indian broad gauge XB class pacific (around 82 tons light) round the sharp curves from the works to the docks. Although a professional, he always had a special love of the locomotive, a fact alluded to in the RCST students' magazine of his day. Together, we toured mainline termini in London and Glasgow where he would identify the different classes of locomotive for me, and point out their features, with explanations of what each component did and how it worked. He was an excellent draughtsman and produced some lovely line drawings for me.

Above: At an SLS dinner in the 1950s.

Seated: At the extreme left, Montague Smith; 5th from the left, George Robin; 7th from the left, David L. Smith; on the extreme right, Alan Dunbar; 5th from the right, Graham Langmuir.

Nearer row standing: 4th from the right, Austin Riley; 5th from right, head, collar and left shoulder only, J. F. McEwan; 6th from the right, John Thomas; 8th from the right, with bow tie, Ronald Nelson; 5th from the left, with glasses, Fred Plant.

Back row: On extreme left, Jim Aird; next to him Donald Stuart.

The second enthusiast I met was the eminent Scottish railway historian John Thomas, for many years a salesman for the Prudential Insurance Company. He was a friend of the family, and long before I was born, regularly visited the Cornwell household in Springburn, my uncle being a school friend of his at Allan Glen's School and sharing his interest in photography. My grandmother told me that, when visiting, he always left her house at a very respectable hour and when she commented on this to him, he would reply "Elders' hours, Mrs Cornwell, Elders' hours!" My mother used to say that John had the whole Scottish railway system and timetable in his head; when asked about how to get to this place or that, he never failed to give full and correct information without having to refer to any printed work.

I saw a lot of John over the years though not, to my everlasting regret, as much as I should have done during the few years before his death. John was always a strong emotional pillar in my life, particularly during my youth. In student days, when things were not going well, it was a great comfort to knock on his door at 240 Gourlay Street, Springburn, and find him at home, ever ready to listen, sympathise and advise. And I was not the only young man in that situation. David Masterton, Alasdair M. Macdonald, Graham Todd and Alastair Harper drew enormous benefit from John's paternal interest in them.

John took me on the Paisley railtour of 1951, run by the Stephenson Locomotive Society (SLS) and hauled by Caley "Jumbo" number 57266. On the train he introduced me to Graham Langmuir whose jointly authored books on the Clyde and West Highland steamers I already had and to whom, therefore, I looked up to with great awe. In later years, the awe, but not the respect diminished somewhat. Graham Langmuir was a senior partner in a Glasgow firm of solicitors, particularly keen on the Caley, and a great authority on coastal shipping. He was a founder member of the Clyde River Steamer Club and served as its third president and its secretary for over 40 years. He had the knack of being able to instantaneously identify any paddle or

Above: Taken about 1950 A3 60073 *St.Gatien* eases out a very heavy Glasgow (Queen St.) King's Cross express. In 150 yards or so the descending gradient towards St. Margarets shed will lighten the A3's task.

turbine steamer or motor vessel in a photograph or slide, easily able to distinguish between almost identical sister-ships. He was tall and handsome, and like so many other enthusiasts I came to know, he was considerate and very helpful, though, on the surface, he appeared rather shy. He was interested in railway preservation and, as solicitor to the Scottish Locomotive Preservation Trust Fund (SLPTF), the owner of the preserved Caley 0-6-0 number 828, gave some very helpful, almost crucial advice, always free of charge. He died in November 1994.

In 1954, John Thomas sponsored my membership of the SLS, though it was not until 1960 that I was able to participate in its activities. At that time, the Glasgow centre of the society met in the now demolished Christian Institute in Bothwell Street. What a wonderful place that was for the young recruit. For there the great and good assembled, T. P. Hally Brown, Chairman of the society, James F. McEwan, at that time very much the father figure of Scottish railway enthusiasts, the almost canonical David L. Smith, the blossoming John Thomas, the entertaining and rumbustious Alan G. Dunbar, that great authority on locomotive performance Ronald I. Nelson and, as I was soon to discover, someone of remarkable scholarship, Montague Smith. These were ably supported by some twenty or so others, notably, George Robin, W.A.C. Smith, Fred A. Plant, Donald H. Stuart, Austin M Riley, Dan McDonald, Douglas McMillan, Wilson Tennent, Dr. Neil McKillop, Alan S.Paterson, Jim B. Aird, Graham King, Ian Coonie, Frank Harvey, George Train and Leslie Callan.

Above: Apart from St. Andrews House replacing the Calton Jail this Eastward panorama remains essentially that described in Robert Lewis Stevensons' "Edinburgh Picturesque Notes" (1878). In 1951, an unidentified A4 approaches on a down express with regulator open within 100 yards of the platform. A large portion of the coaches are still on the 1 in 200 incline up from St. Margarets. A3 No. 60041 *Salmon Trout* simmers away at a suburban platform.

Thomas Peter Hally Brown, or Hally as he was known to his friends, was a chartered accountant and senior figure in the Boy Scouts movement. Handsome and well built, he had considerable charm and simply exhumed bonhomie. He owned a model railway based on the London & South Western Railway (LSWR) and had even lectured on the Drummond locomotives of the LSWR in its home territory. After 12 years as Chairman of the SLS, he was elected as one of its Vice-Presidents. He was interested in preservation and, along with Graham Langmuir, Lt-Commander James Black and Sir Peter Allen provided crucial support in securing Caley number 828 for posterity when all seemed lost. He was a very early supporter of the Strathspey Railway but died in August 1978, only weeks after the granting of its Light Railway Order.

James F. McEwan (Jim to many) worked with the steel factors Barnes and Bell. He had an encyclopaedic knowledge of many aspects of Scottish railways, particularly the Caledonian and the North British and was also knowledgeable on the Great Northern of Ireland. He was one of the few men I ever met, perhaps the only one, who never failed to answer a question; he seemed to have expert knowledge or experience of every facet of the Caledonian and North British railways and was clearly familiar too with the industries they served. He was a strong supporter of the Boys' Brigade and always ready to help the young enthusiast hungry for information. He was made a Vice-President of the SLS in 1957 and was a founder member of the Caledonian Railway Association and contributor to the latter's journal, "The True Line". Despite the high esteem in which he was held as a major railway historian, he was a humble man and not averse to 'small talk'. Latterly he lived in a house overlooking Glasgow University's Garscube estate, which housed the Faculty of Veterinary Medicine where I worked, and he would from time to time converse with me about some of the animals grazing there. Following his death in December 1991, George Robin wrote: "Yes, wasn't Jim McEwan one of the world's best? He certainly proved a great friend to me when I took over from him the Secretaryship of the Scottish Area of the SLS and many are the kindness he has shown me since".

In the 1940s, Jim wrote a long and highly detailed serial article on the Locomotives of the Caledonian Railway, (in the Locomotive, Railway Carriage & Wagon Review, published by the Locomotive Publishing Company) from its formation until the end of the Lambie period. Unfortunately, however, official documents and drawings were not nearly so accessible then as they are now, and current research has revealed a number of mistakes, especially on the Drummond locomotives. Nevertheless, his magnum opus contained a wealth of information on the Sinclair, Conner and Brittain eras, which, but for Jim's industry, would probably not be available to us today.

David L. Smith was a truly unique individual, not only in his particular approach to railway history but also in his great literary gifts. Who else would have thought of describing Whithorn station and its track layout as "not at all like Waterloo"? As a raconteur, whether at meetings or privately with friends, he had no equal, though John Thomas at his best perhaps came close. This was because he had a keen sense of the dramatic and, when telling a story, would accompany the narrative with appropriate body language, frowns, grimaces, gesticulations and waves of the arms. Moreover, he went through the same 'act' every time he told the same story and the language - including the pauses for dramatic effect - would also be the same on each occasion, as though it was part of a prescribed text written down in his head.

David was born in Dalmellington, Ayrshire, in 1899 and seldom enjoyed good health. He was quite tall but slim and, during the twenty odd years I knew him, always appeared physically fragile. Looking back, my picture of him is of a very thin edition of Pope John Paul II. He moved to Ayr in 1926 where he was employed in the County Council's Library, in which he rose to the position of Deputy Chief Librarian. He was most at home when talking to railwaymen and his approach to railway history was based on his conversations with the older men, especially the older enginemen. So it was seldom a matter just of engines but nearly always of 'engines and men'. He was a very humble man and wrote of his alarm when he first discovered that the SLS was representing him to its members as the authority on the Glasgow & South Western Railway (GSWR) - which he certainly was. But he was by no means parochial and visited several foreign countries including the United States, where he enjoyed a footplate trip on a New York Central Hudson driven at 80mph on full regulator and 65% cut-off. As he said, "now that was an engine!"

David was unstinting in the help which he offered to others, particularly to us young 'apprentices'. In the early 1960s, I was keen to get more information on the Manson 4-4-0s and David obliged by sending me full details, ie numbers, dates of construction and withdrawal, renumberings, rebuilding and shed allocations of every engine of each of the four classes. These details were listed in pencil in the neatest imaginable way in his own exquisite handwriting. And there was much more he sent me besides these.

Right: The first non-stop Kings Cross to Edinburgh service to be introduced after the war was "The Capitals Limited" on 23 May 1949. Just as it would have been in LNER days, Longniddry Junction has all the ingredients of earlier times. The down non-stop "Capitals Limited" of probably 1950 had only another 13.5 miles to go behind A4 60029 *Woodcock* before reaching the northern capital.

Left: Pounding through the same station in 1951 and leaning with the curve, A2 No 60536 *Trimbush* hauls "The Flying Scotsman". Why, whenever I photographed this train, did it never have the headboard up?

When I first got to know him, David was living in a hotel in Ayr. I remember visiting him one summer and being shocked to discover that, because of the influx of summer holidaymakers, he had been transferred to the annex, all his worldly possessions having to be accommodated in one small single room. It was therefore with great relief that his friends heard of his forthcoming marriage to Margaret, an ideal partner who radiated both warmth and down-to-earth confidence. John Thomas was the first to know. David, who could be very solemn at times, took him aside to ask him to be his best man. "John, I'm thinking of changing my way of life", he began. But before he could get any further, John chipped in "Davie, don't tell me you're giving up the Sou-west for the Caley!"

As well as articles in the SLS Journal and in commercial magazines, David published five major books. They were compulsive reading; George Train told me that he just could not put down David's book on the Dalmellington Iron Company and its locomotives and sat up all night reading it. My own special favourite is the very last paragraph of 'Tales of the GSWR' which never fails to bring tears to my eyes. David died in February 1985.

Alan G. Dunbar was a professional railwayman. He was born in Bucksburn, Aberdeen, in 1902 and always retained his rich Aberdeen accent and love of the old Great North of Scotland Railway (GNSR). He moved with his parents to Maryhill, Glasgow, in 1916 and found employment in the stores department and, soon afterwards, in the analytical laboratory in Cowlairs works. Pressurised into going to technical college, which he didn't want to do, he instead obtained an apprenticeship at St. Rollox works. On completion of that, he became a fitter at Balornock shed but later transferred to the LNER, first at Eastfield shed, then Parkhead as chargehand fitter and finally to Polmont as foreman.

Alan had a lifelong love affair with the steam locomotive and took every opportunity to record all that was going on around him and, whenever possible, to delve into the past. His historical research was two-pronged. Firstly, David L. Smith - like, he collected stories from old enginemen, especially the former driver Jock McLeish of Perth who had a fund of information on Caley 'engines and men'. Much of this he published in the Ian Allan press. Secondly, facilitated by K.R.M. Cameron (who finished his career as Motive Power Superintendent of the Scottish Region of BR), he studied redundant official documents and records from the Caley locomotive department. He was responsible for the preservation of much official material which he later donated to the National Archives of Scotland in Edinburgh.

Alan was a kindly and generous man who made much of the information he had gathered available to others, including myself. He was a good and true friend and I owe a lot to him. But I feel that there was something of the frustrated academic in him. He wanted to be a good historian but his enthusiasm occasionally led him into publishing something he had not thoroughly thought through. But that is part of the human condition to which all of us, including myself, are susceptible and without Alan's tremendous research commitment, we would have a much poorer understanding of Caley locomotive history than we would currently possess.

Another of Alan's characteristics was that he liked to be provocative, making statements and voicing opinions that he knew would be controversial and stimulate debate. A case in point was the argument in the SLS Journal between himself as supporter of the Caley 140 class and Ken Hoole as advocate for the North Eastern Railway R class, as to which did the better work. Strangely, both men died within a few weeks of each other but not, I hasten to add, due to that particular debate.

Alan was a founder member of the Caledonian Railway Association and was unanimously elected its first President, a much-deserved reward for his many years of service, both to the Caledonian Railway Company and to its memory and reputation. He died in January 1989.

I don't think that Ronald Nelson and I ever had occasion to speak to each other, so I cannot say much about him, other than that he regularly attended meetings, was always smartly attired in a suit with double-breasted jacket and often smoked a cigar, as befitted a very successful publisher and businessman. He seemed a very pleasant but quiet sort of chap, usually sitting in the front row and listening thoughtfully to the speaker. On one occasion Alan Pegler was the guest speaker. I remember him going up to Ronald Nelson and excitedly telling him "I have bought Flying Scotsman", to which Ronald Nelson replied "and I have bought Merlin!" Clearly, something must have upset his plans. At that time BR was quite indifferent, some would say hostile, to the preservation movement. On another occasion, C. Hamilton Ellis was the guest speaker. Before the start of his address, Ronald Nelson approached him with the news "I had a wonderful run behind a Deltic last week." The guest's response was unlikely to have been what he expected; "well at least we can be thankful that Dr. Diesel fell overboard and was drown in the North Sea!"

Through commercial publications as well as through the SLS Journal, the above names were well known to me in 1960 but I had never heard of Montague Smith until he read a paper on the locomotives of Matthew Holmes. It was a complete eye-opener to me for I had never before heard so much technical detail. In the discussion which followed, a chap very much of my own age, Graham King, asked a question about the tender axlebox bearings of the Holmes engines and a short debate on this took place between speaker and questioner. Both were clearly masters of the subject. I went away feeling very small but with a strong ambition to learn a lot more. There was much food for thought. At first I tended to assume that the Holmes

Above: Journey's end at about 9.20 a.m. for A2/3 No. 518 *Tehran* on the 1.00 a.m. ex King's Cross service which included sleeping cars which could be occupied from about 11 p.m. in London, luxury! The suburban platform was employed so keeping the main station clear for up expresses around 10 a.m.

locomotives, or maybe North British locomotives as a whole, were the speaker's speciality but I soon found out that he was equally conversant with the locomotives of each of the other four Scottish railways. There is no doubt in my mind that he was the supreme authority on the design features of all the Scottish pre-grouping locomotives.

Montague Smith was always "Monty" to his friends but liked the formal title Montague Smith Junior because both his father and his paternal grandfather, church organists, choirmasters and composers of church music, shared the same names. He was a small thin man with narrow balding head and pronounced lips. Like David L. Smith, he had never enjoyed good health; he used to say that he had "a chist (chest) like a bad-steaming 4F", not a popular engine with Caley men at the best of times. He was a professional photographer by training but,

as a result of poor health, was never in employment for very long. Fortunately, there was enough money in the family for him to scrape by. His maternal grandfather had been a doctor in Dennistoun and had a holiday home in Kirn on the Cowal coast. In his youth, Monty spent many holidays in Kirn and got to know the Clyde steamers and, in particular, their engines and engineers very well indeed. In later years, he had the freedom of the engine-room platform of the remaining Clyde paddle steamers and was an authority on reversing engines and other steam-operated ancillary equipment.

The Smith family also made their holidays regularly in the Biggar area and Monty spent much of his time on the Peebles branch. There, through the benevolence of driver Hugh Wilson, he learned to drive a locomotive and, in due course, became intimate with many of the Carstairs enginemen

Above: Such stuff as dreams are made of – the Waverley Station atmosphere, 1964.

working the branch. One happy result is the extensive and comprehensive photographic portrayal he made of the branch.

Monty lived in a very large ground floor flat in a Victorian red sandstone tenement on the corner of Rupert Street and West Princes Street in Glasgow. The house was never modernised or refurbished, the lounge still containing a grand piano and small organ, not to mention his father's pipes on a rack beside the fireplace. Meetings of various committees were often held in the dining room but business was frequently interrupted by his insistence on revealing some telling point quite unrelated to the agenda. Then, about three-quarters of an hour after the start of the meeting, his mother and sister would come in with the supper and sit down round the table with us. His mother was fairly deaf, and while Monty was laying off about Drummond, she would be loudly inviting us "to take plenty". Always in

attendance at the meetings was Monty's budgie 'Fergus MacIvor Vich Ian Vohr', whom one was expected to greet with a few suitable words. No, we didn't get through much business but I wouldn't have missed these occasions for the entire world! Incidentally, after the great highland chief's death, Monty bought another two budgies and named them Dugald and Peter in honour of the Drummond brothers who were his greatest heroes. During his last years, Monty would rent a furnished room in Port Bannatyne on the island of Bute for a month of the summer. Onto the train and steamer with him would go the said Dugald and Peter in one large cage.

Monty was blessed with a photographic memory, which enabled him to make good use of the many technical journals in Glasgow's marvellous Mitchell Library. During the war, he wrote to Edward Thompson to request that copies of NBR and GNSR locomotive drawings be made available

to him. Thompson replied that that was not the LNER's normal practice but that, in this case, he would instruct the Cowlairs drawing office to provide him with copies of certain drawings. In the 1960s and 1970s, Monty spent many hours in the Cowlairs drawing office, which, by then, was the only one still functional in the Scottish Region. Around that time, Robert Cogger was collecting official drawings for the national collection in the old Clapham Transport Museum and those not selected by him were made available to other museums, societies and a few individuals. Monty was able to amass a very large collection of these drawings, now in the possession of the National Archives of Scotland, and these he studied in great depth. Although without formal engineering qualifications, he had an extremely good grasp of anything technical.

While Monty's knowledge of Scottish steam locomotive engineering was unsurpassed, his judgement was sometimes adversely affected by a strong tendency to bias. Having said that, I must admit that on occasions I was taken aback by his lack of bias, as for example when he forcefully insisted that the work of the Great Eastern Railway's 4-4-0s was as good as that of the Caley's. On one famous occasion, after a debacle with steam, he volunteered that the diesel locomotive substituting for the failed steam engine had done very well indeed. He had a dry sense of humour and, on the occasion of the above-mentioned debacle, when a J37 was in trouble for steam and running hot bearings, remarked that "everything was heating except for the firebox".

Like those already mentioned, Monty was always ready to help the enquirer and exceedingly generous in the photographs and drawings he handed out. But one had to be careful with him because he had a fairly thin skin and could react strongly against criticism, either of himself or of his heroes. Through this he fell out with several of his friends. In the end, it was all rather sad He was another frustrated academic who had collected an enormous amount of information on the locomotives of all five Scottish railways but chose those of the

GSWR as the subject for a book. His highly detailed manuscript was clearly unsuitable for commercial publication as it stood but there was no way of changing it without borrowing from David L. Smith, whose book on GSWR locomotives was already in print. Without the financial resources for a private publication, he endeavoured to find someone willing to sponsor it but all was in vain. Fortunately, his manuscript is now in the hands of Stuart Rankin of the GSWR Association. He died in May 1992.

Donald R Stuart was a professional engineer who had graduated from Cambridge University and then become one of the last London & North Western Railway (LNWR) pupils at Crewe Works. He was very proud of his LNWR origins and an authority on its locomotives. He later became Assistant Chief Mechnical Engineer for the Burma Railways but, following the Japanese invasion, escaped to India, passage of the jungle being made with his daughter on his back. In 1942 he was appointed Works Manager at the carriage shops of the Bengal and Assam Railway. After the war, he returned to Britain to join Rendal, Palmer and Tritton and was closely involved with the closure of the NBL Company in 1962, as a result of which he managed to acquire and transfer to the Mitchell Library a large number of photographs and other records.

Donald was a tall man who frequently dressed in what looked like corduroy breeches with knee-high woollen stockings, thick woollen sweater and heavy boots. The number of his house near Hillfoot station on the Milngavie branch was denoted by part of a LNWR locomotive numberplate and near his front door was a station lamp and seat

Left: A4 60029 *Woodcock* really making a dash for it on the up "The Capitals Limited" between Longniddry and Drem during the early 1950s. The sporting name of Woodcock was given to this engine in LNER days whilst numbered 4493.

Right: Once again A4 60031 *Golden Plover* gets away in great style through the Edinburgh suburbs at Joppa on a Sunday Waverley to Kings Cross express about 1954.

Bottom: In the mid 1950's A4 60031 *Golden Plover* has full command of the down "Flying Scotsman" at Aberlady junction and only another fifteen miles left to go and journeys end for today. The old North British branch to Aberlady and Gullane left the mainline here, although passenger traffic had left the branch twenty years earlier in 1932.

from, if I remember correctly, the closed station at Blanefield. His living room contained a huge table, usually completely covered in railway drawings, photographs and other documents. Mounted on his mantelpiece was the curved nameplate of a LNWR locomotive. When he offered tea, it was scalding hot and served up in the largest mug I have ever seen. His special interest was in Buddicom and the early Crewe-type locomotives but he was indefatigable in all he undertook, not least in dispelling the myth of Box Tunnel and Brunel's birthday. He was a kindly and generous man, ever ready to help others, and in every way the perfect gentleman. He died in December 1977.

Alan J. S. Paterson was considerably younger than the aforementioned men were. A chartered accountant that stepped into his father's practice, with an office overlooking Glasgow's George Square, he had a lifelong love affair with railway and steamer research and writing. Indeed, one

Left: Portobello station was worth a visit and especially so on 20 June 1951 when "The Queen of Scots" was expected. Owing to an engine failure at the border K3/3 No 61875 was commandeered and the Pullman ran only twenty-five minutes late.

Right: Further out from Edinburgh, the same train running to time was hauled by an immaculate A1 60116 *Hal O' The Wynd* in blue livery. Those were the days! For the record, D30 Scott No 2417 on former North British metals also carried that wonderful name.

In Sir Walter Scott's novel "The Fair Maids of Perth" Henry Smith – the finest armourer between the Tay and Venice – was known as Hal o' the Wynd (Wynd meaning lane). He married Catherine Glover, The Fair Maid.

Above: The down "Flying Scotsman" hauled by A4 60004 *William Whitelaw* at Portobello South Junction in 1951. The tracks going off to the right are those of the Waverley route to Carlisle via Hawick. In the background an ex NBR J36 trundles a goods train from Leith towards a fly-over crossing the main line, before joining it further east. The wagon in the foreground stored coal for the comfort of the signalmen in the nearby box.

Below: On another occasion A2 No 60536 *Trimbush* was captured on the down "Flying Scotsman" loaded to thirteen coaches on the Portobello Station avoiding line about 1951, when she seems to have been regularly rostered on this turn.

sometimes wondered when he had time for his professional work. His particular approach was to go through old newspapers and journals in the Mitchell and other public reference libraries. Along with Graham King, he took notes on the condition, i.e. motion details, type of boiler and tender etc. of pre-grouping locomotives seen in numerous shed visits and meticulously recorded these, together with boiler numbers and the inscriptions on tender number and capacity plates. He was very ambitious in all he undertook, always ready to talk about his research and eager, I think, to be acknowledged as a major locomotive and steamer historian. His enthusiasms, however, tended to change from one subject to another at intervals of three or four years. His NBR "period" was followed by the first of his Clyde steamer "periods", then by fairly long spell on Caley locomotives, before returning to

Left: V1s, V3s or C16s usually hauled suburban and local services around the capital. Later as the Ivatt 2-6-0's arrived they were ideal for the purpose too.

Bottom Left: The V1 on the North Berwick run was always spick and span and when allocated there, pre-war, was the pride of its North Berwick crew. As seen here on a local to Edinburgh. This service very often ran right through to Corstophine Terminus to the west of Edinburgh.

Bottom Right: In 1951, an ex North British C16 class tank, approaching Portobello off the Waverley route hauling a short distance local.

Above: The up "Queen of Scots" on the through road at Portobello, A3 60090 *Grand Parade* is in charge. An ex NBR J37 shunts in what was a busy yard in 1951. Originally named as the Harrogate Pullman when introduced in the summer of 1923. As the new timetable was introduced for the summer of 1928, the timing of the train was improved and the journey extended to Glasgow Queen Street, and the name Queen of Scots was adopted. On the declaration of war in September 1939, the service was suspended along with all other Pullman services in the country. As peace returned in 1945 the Queen of Scots was not reinstated, this would not come until after the demise of the LNER and the 5 July 1948, the first summer of the new British Railways. The timings of this prestige Pullman service were to change as the 1950s progressed, becoming gradually easier. Finally British Railways dropped the service altogether from Saturday 13 June 1964.

CROSS THE RAILWAY BY THE BRIDGE ONLY

Opposite: An unidentified up express entering Joppa station, which apart from the signals, seems little changed since North British Railway days. Disturbing the peace is one of Arthur Henry Peppercorn's A1 Pacifics 60151 appropriately named *Midlothian* in 1951.

Right: One of Gresley's earlier design of Pacifics A3 No 2745 *Captain Cuttle* passing Craigentinny carriage sidings in 1938 with the down Thames-Forth express comprising LMS stock and an ex NBR carriage next to the locomotive, probably added at Carlisle. In the background stands a newly repainted ex NBR 6 wheel brake and a clerestory vehicle of NER origin.

Bottom Right: 1938 and everything in sight is still ex NBR property. The 0-4-4 tank engine now LNER class G9 No 9351 on pilot work makes some gentle smoke and also acting as the standby locomotive for the delightful Polton branch. To the left of No 9351 is a non-corridor suburban and to the right, an express passenger coach.

Clyde steamers. The Caley was undoubtedly his favourite railway though he did have a brief flirtation with the Great Western. Much of his research on Caley locomotives was published in the SLS Journal and in the Ian Allan press, he contributed to the Regional Railway History series published by David & Charles and wrote three magnificent books on the Clyde steamers. As the first secretary of the SLPTF, he put a great deal of work into publicity and fund-raising for the preservation of Caley number 828. He learned Gaelic and, for a while sang in a Gaelic choir, but suffered a number of serious and tragic health-problems and died in 2001.

Mention of Clyde steamers reminds me that people with nautical interests or background were quite common among us. In addition to Graham Langmuir and Alan Paterson, there were Dan McDonald, Captain A. Rodger, Lt.-Commander James Black RNR, Graham King, Dr. Neil McKillop, John Thomas, George Train and Leslie Callan. Dan McDonald was the authority on Clyde puffers and on much of Clyde shipbuilding, a tall and quiet man with Roman nose, bright pink cheeks and a ginger toupee. Captain Rodger's appearance perhaps belied his calling because, though always dressed in a smart suit and in every way a charming and polished gentleman, he had obtained his master's ticket by rounding the horn in a sailing ship. 'The Commander' had served in HMS Resolution during the war, had a great love for the LNWR and owned a gauge 1 LNWR model railway in his loft. He was the second chairman of the SLPTF and a founding director of the Strathspey Railway Company. Graham King was a graduate engineer with experience of work in the shipyards, while Dr. McKillop, John Thomas, George Train and Leslie Callan were Clyde steamer enthusiasts. Graham King served for many years as secretary of the SLPTF and is presently engineering director of the Strathspey Railway. In the 1960s, he photographed the inside motion of many pre-grouping locomotives, his resulting collection of photographs forming a unique and most important archive. He also, has built some beautiful five inch gauge live steam locomotives, including a Highland Railway "Loch" with working vacuum brake. Dr. Neil McKillop was a real character. He had become a railway enthusiast almost by chance while attending school in Bridge of Allan; excused from sports, he had wandered down to the station one day and been invited by the signalman to inspect the box. That incident was the beginning of a life-long interest in railways. After graduating in medicine, he practised in London and Manchester before returning home to Glasgow. He never had a car but visited his patients by public transport; I met him one day on a Clyde steamer sailing from Gourock to Dunoon. He was on his way to visit two elderly patients; I hope they paid him well. Neil was the first chairman of the SLPTF and raised a considerable amount of money for it by selling photographs of locomotives and Clyde steamers. He died in June 2004. George Train was an actuary, a trustee of the SLPTF, and a founder member of the Coastal Cruising Association. Later on, he was heavily involved in the preservation of PS Waverley.

Right: K3/3 No 61884 on a down goods nearing Prestonpans. Such traffic to the west or north of Edinburgh was routed via the southern arc of the suburban railway. Goods traffic for Leith travelled directly through Portobello.

Many of us also had a special affection for the Glasgow trams. Most prominent among these were Douglas McMillan, progressman in the erecting shop in Cowlairs Works, and Wilson Tennent, an engine driver on the narrow gauge railway in Provan Gas Works, both of whom were recognised as authorities on trams, or cars as they were called in Glasgow. Ian Coonie, another keen tram enthusiast, was an authority on the Belfast and County Down Railway but was also very interested in the railways of the USA. Austin Riley, who lived in Paisley and had written articles on the LMS standard locomotives for the SLS Journal during the Stanier era, was a keen cricket fan and travelled to London every year for the test matches at Lords and The Oval. He played an important role socially by organising a high tea in Miss Buick's Restaurant after every SLS meeting in Glasgow. The management was very tolerant, arranging for some 12 to 20 of us to sit round one long table and allowing us to remain until 'closing time'. As a result, friendships were made and bonds strengthened.

I cannot conclude this account without reference to three others. George Robin was an 'elder statesman' of the society and a much respected authority on the geography, history and operation of railways in Glasgow and the West of Scotland. Years later, I had the honour of teaching his son, also George and happily following in his father's footsteps as a railway enthusiast, in Glasgow University. W.A.C. Smith had similar interests and expertise and must have photographed every station and signal box in the region. Much is owed to both of them. Fred Plant was a solicitor who lived in Greenock and was

the authority on engine workings and performance on the Prince's Pier, Gourock and Wemyss Bay lines. He was frequently to be seen talking to the engine crews or on the footplate at the end of a run and, from his attire and attitude, looked much more like a locomotive inspector than a solicitor. He took many locomotive photographs in the Glasgow and Greenock areas.

I realise that there were a number of others whom I have not mentioned and beg their indulgence.

My attendance became somewhat erratic from around 1966 and there were several, such as Len Wilkins, Ken MacKay and Jim Shepherd who were becoming very active about that time. I was a member of several other railway societies, each with its own 'characters' and, from 1972, became heavily involved in the Strathspey Railway. I therefore got to know many other enthusiasts but that must remain another matter.

Just Waverley

Below: It is an indication of the volume of traffic handled by a station when locomotives are received from the MPD in groups. Coupled up and about to enter the Mound tunnel are A4 No 9 *Union of South Africa* for the 2pm to Aberdeen service, V1 No 7660 with head board for Hyndland and A2/3 No 519 *Honeyway* for the 2pm to Glasgow.

Opposite: A 1938 line up at Waverley. A4 No 4482 *Golden Eagle* ready for the 2pm express to Aberdeen, being inspected by a gentleman in a kilt. Adjacent are two unidentified Pacifics, one on the 2pm express to Glasgow Queen Street, the other Pacific will follow the Aberdeen train with an express to Perth.

Opposite: A4 No 4485 *Kestrel* and A4 No 4490 *Empire of India* wait their turns of duty. Little road traffic is in evidence on the Waverley Bridge that day in 1937. The fine Edwardian building, the North British Station Hotel in the background with the clock tower is partly obscured by locomotive exhaust. It was said that the clock was set two or three minutes early, to ensure that passengers on Princes Street caught their trains on time.

Right: To the uninitiated or an observer without a timetable, surprises abounded. D49 No 2733 *Northumberland* in wartime livery and rather dirty is heading in for duty. The unidentified Scottish Director D11 on the North Road bursts out of the Mound tunnel, keeping up with a Gresley V1 No 7624 on local stopping service for the west or on the suburban circle.

Bottom Right: Gentler activity when J83 No 8481 and V1 No 7659 shunt stock at the Mound Tunnel. The lining and Gill Sans lettering suggest the J83 has acquired LNER green in place of the previous black livery. No 8481 is probably handling a few fish vans off a recently arrived express from Aberdeen.

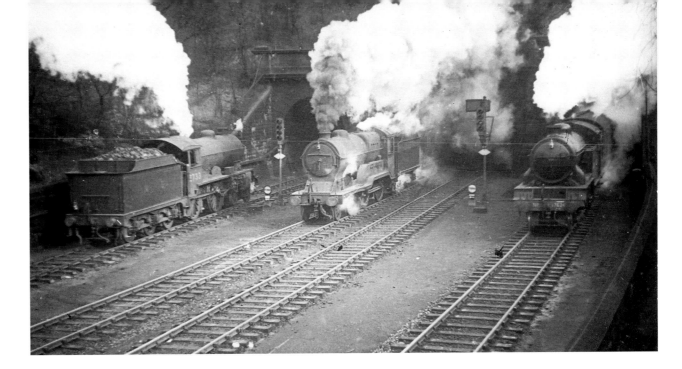

Above: A beautiful crisp day in 1947, the renumbered and repainted A4 No 9 *Union of South Africa* and still in full LNER turnout, shows just how Haymarket MPD could look after a locomotive, even down to the burnished buffers and coupling. The buildings of Princes Street are hidden in the exhaust of No 9 and the steam of a locomotive waiting for signal clearance. The streamliner just escapes from the shadow of the castle on the late afternoon express for the north-east conveying through coaches from the down "Flying Scotsman". Railway enthusiasts, now and in the future, owe an everlasting debt of gratitude to Alan Pegler and John Cameron who preserved 4472 *Flying Scotsman* and 4488 *Union of South Africa* linking, by happy coincidence, Kings Cross and Haymarket MPD, and their capital Cities.

Bottom Left: To see the latest Pacific a visit to Waverley and the arrival, about 1.30pm of an incoming express from over the border, could be a rewarding experience. Just off such a roster a very new British Railways A2 No E527 *Sun Chariot* makes towards the MPD. This photograph was taken very early in 1948.

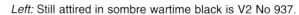

Left: Still attired in sombre wartime black is V2 No 937.

Below Left: The benefit of at least full lettering is applied to a black A3 No 100 *Spearmint* in 1946.

Below Right: A touch of the 1939 *pizzazz* with A4 No 4482 *Golden Eagle.*

Right: These were the times when excessive railway activity called for a split second decision. Gresley A4 No 9 *Union of South Africa* and Thompson A2/3 No 519 *Honeyway* back up into the Mound tunnel, preceded by an unidentified locomotive, but just showing the 'Hyndland' destination board. Leaving at the same time was Gresley D49 No 2725 *Inverness-shire* in post war grime. At least some of the coaches are fresh from refurbishment, a few more times in the tunnels and they too will match the engine. This was most likely the 1.16pm Fife express along the coastal route terminating in Crail.

Below Right: The 10.20am ex Aberdeen express gave observing enthusiasts a thrill when it pulled into Waverley at 1.52pm, as two coaches carried 'Aberdeen - Penzance' destination boards. The vehicles went forward via York and Swindon, reaching their terminus the following morning at 7.30am. Sleeping cars were available from Swindon for the comfort of passengers. Remarkably this service was introduced as long ago as 1921. Gresley designed and built new stock for this marathon journey in 1939. They were little used as intended, when the through coaches were discontinued at the outbreak of the Second World War. Fitted with a stepped tender V2 No 4811 draws into Waverley on this roster in 1938.

Left: A discriminating and sophisticated traveller expressed it once as "almost a pleasure to be able to admire a railway line, exceptionally quiet and well behaved as is Edinburgh's garden railway, for the railway is to Edinburgh what the Grand Canal is to the Venetians, who would probably be pleased to exchange the canal for the railway". On an incoming express from Glasgow (Queen Street), where once the Nor' Loch filled the ravine beneath the castle, A3 No 43 *Brown Jack* slips quietly through the gardens in 1947.

Bottom Left: Another of the fine A3s No 57 *Ormonde* rounds the foot of the castle and is about to plunge into Haymarket tunnel en route to Glasgow (Queen Street). From this point the Nor' Loch spread out eastward. It was really a moat artificially created in 1460 to protect the North side of the Old Town by damming up the Craig Burn. Mention of the canal by our traveller is not so far fetched. On draining the Loch in 1820 consideration was given to extending the canal from Glasgow along the line of the present railway. This proposal was not a serious contender and the gardens were planned, so returning the land to its pre 1460 use when it was known as the King's Garden. In agreement with our traveller who believed it is too late to complain now, "Venice must keep the canal and Edinburgh the railway. It is better thus and none should regret it".

Right: The additional traffic following the opening of the Forth and Tay Bridges (in 1887 and 1890 respectively) served to increase the already congested conditions round Edinburgh. Quadrupling the track from Saughton to Portobello with additional tunnels and considerable alterations at Waverley Station solved the problem. In the Spring of 1947 an unlined black B1 No 1076 emerges from the Haymarket tunnel with a train from Perth. This additional bore and trackwork obviously encroached onto St. Cuthbert's churchyard and burial ground and Princes Street gardens but not without local protest. In the process the station however acquired more plantform space than in any other British station except Waterloo.

Below: By chance during the early months of 1948 these two B1s shared a unique distinction as I caught them in Princes Street Gardens. Built at NBL. Co in Glasgow No 1263 entered service fully lined out and numbered in LNER green livery on 3 December 1947. No 1061 entered Cowlairs Works on 5 December 1947 in its original unlined black livery for repairs and emerged on 27 December 1947 in full LNER green glory. Few other locomotives could have been turned closer to Nationalisation Day as LNER engines after this pair of B1s on 1 January 1948.

The Caley

Below: When the citizens of Edinburgh's thoughts turned to a highland journey, their starting point would have been the Caledonian Railway station. This was situated at the West End of Princes Street, the opposite end of the thoroughfare from the Waverley. Stirling, Perth, Inverness and beyond or Callander and Oban could be their destination. The industrial heartland of England (Birmingham, Manchester, and Liverpool) was also well served from this station, known locally as the Caley. So too was Wales or the West Country for the more adventurous. Then there were the Royal and Mid-day Scots to Euston and sleeping car services to the South. The Royal Scot portion from Edinburgh usually consisted of only five coaches but included a dining car, which joined the main Glasgow portion at Symington. At holiday times, as here during Easter 1938, a full train was required, hauled by an unidentified Jubilee class locomotive, piloted by a Compound carrying the old CR destination sign above the buffer-beam indicating mainline route south.

Right: Jubilee class No 5646 *Napier* and Compound No 1145 in 1939 apparently only moving stock about the station.

Below: Black 5 No 5083 ready for a stopping train duty on the main line south in the summer of 1939.

Bottom Right: A real ex CR Locomotive in the 'Caley', LMS No 14434 was formerly No 894 of the Caledonian Railway and an example of McIntosh's Dunalastair III class glimpsed in 1937.

Left: The route indicator on Compound No 901 shows its next duty will be to the North – probably Perth via Stirling, nearby, "The Mid-Day Scot" vehicles are ready for their passengers in 1937. The engine will have given thirteen years service already at this point and was a fine design from Midland Railway days, before the Grouping when George Hughes became the first Chief Mechanical Engineer of the newly formed London Midland & Scottish Railway in 1923.

Bottom Left: Without the modern semaphore signals, one might have been back in the glorious days of the Caledonian Railway. During 1958, The "Festival Special" was a promotional train for journalists in connection with the Edinburgh International Festival of Music and Drama. Here, entering Princes Street station, is the locomotive famous for its performance in the railway race to Scotland in 1888. Both locomotive and coaches were in full CR livery. What a colourful place the station must have been pre-1923. The final flourish for this occasion was the driver's splendid Victorian beard of theatrical origin.

Right: With Glasgow Central only forty six miles away, long distance express locomotives arriving there could usefully be employed on fill-in duties to Edinburgh (1938). Royal Scot No 6105 *Cameron Highlander* awaits departure while No 6124 *London Scottish* (allocated to Crewe North) reverses to Dalry Loco shed after being relieved of its incoming stock. There was even a regular visit of a streamlined Pacific about this time and only slightly less glamorous Duchess Pacifics at a later date.

Bottom Right: Workmanlike is Black Five 44994 during 1958 hauling the late afternoon express for Manchester and Liverpool, photographed passing 64C Dalry Road locomotive depot on the left. Beyond the water tank, the lines can be seen diverging for the North. The station serving this area closed in 1962 and the engine shed closed completely on 3 October 1965.

Merrie Carlisle Weekend

Top Left: This mecca needs no recommendation for the rich photographic pickings to be had in the Citadel station. The first four photographs, taken between 3 and 4pm on a summer's day in 1938, prove the point. They were chosen from five consecutive negatives. How many miles would one travel today for such a haul? At 3.13pm, the down Thames-Forth Express arrived, drawn by LMS Black Five No 5151. LNER A3 No 2748 *Colorado* is ready to take the train forward on the Waverley route to Edinburgh at 3.18pm.

Bottom Left: At 3.15pm sharp, the Coronation Scot sweeps into the station from Glasgow, believed to be hauled by No 6223 *Princess Alice*. A two-minute stop was allocated to take up passengers only and for a change of engine crew. Incidentally, the up and down "Coronation Scots" were booked to pass Preston at 4.45pm and 4.44pm respectively.

Top Right: At 3.40pm the rostored ex NBR Atlantic No 9875 *Midlothian* would take forward a stopping all stations train to Edinburgh. Just think if the Roman name had been retained that splendid LMS station sign would have announced Luguvallium. The castle in the background dates from the Norman times and was captured by Bonnie Prince Charlie in 1745. This was the second time this border city castle had been surrendered to the Scots; the first was after a yearlong siege in 1645. But all appears peaceful on this sunny afternoon.

Bottom Right: At 3.52pm the up Mid-day Scot sends a resounding bark upwards as it departs with Stanier's first Pacific No 6200 *The Princess Royal* in charge. This service includes through coaches from Aberdeen, Edinburgh and Stranraer Harbour, conveient and well patronised for a good run south.

Top Left: In all this excitement it is not surprising that the fifth consecutive negative referred to, was a double exposure – of "The Coronation Scot" and "The Royal Scot" – and it still hurts to this day. The next day, in poorer light, the down "Royal Scot" hauled by a very new Pacific, probably No 6231 *Duchess of Atholl*, sets off north at 3pm, with her reporting numbers obscuring her true identity.

Bottom Left: On a brief visit to Kingmoor shed, the ex LNWR Cauliflower was discovered. Although not in steam she was obviously still in service, bringing her distinct North Western style to a Caledonian Railway engine shed. The ex North British Railway shed at Canal or the ex London & North Western Railway's own shed at Upperby would also tempt visitors to this border city.

Off Towards the North

Right: A2/3 No 60519 *Honeyway* climbs from Bridge of Earn to Glenfarg on a Perth-Edinburgh Express via the Forth Bridge. This more direct North British Railway route from Edinburgh through Kinross was to close in the so called rationalisation of the Sixties, leaving the traveller of the 21st century to be forced to explore this beautiful rolling countryside by car. The route allowed the traveller to reach Cowdenbeath once dubbed the Chicago of Fife as its population kept on doubling every ten years between 1850 and the outbreak of the First World War, as people flocked to the town to find work in the coal seams.

Top Left and Below: Gresley P2 2-8-2 No 2002 *Earl Marischal* pauses at Stonehaven on the 7.35am ex Waverley. At this time, through sleeping cars from Kings Cross on "The Night Scotsman "were taken forward to Aberdeen. After the thrill of an illicit run in the cab, I had to return to my seat on the train in case a bowler-hatted Inspector was on the platform at the terminus.

Bottom Right: Another of these fabulous P2s No 2006 *Wolf of Badenoch* enters Waverley East having brought its own stock up from Craigentinny sidings and entering the suburban platforms. The coaches included an Aberdeen based dining car and as the day was a Sunday perhaps this was an excursion returning to the Granite City.

Right: To the enthusiast, the P2 class represented something special, as indeed it was. All kinds of criticism, be they true or false were levelled at the class and resulted in the rebuilding of the six locomotives as Pacifics. Now classified A2/2 and numbered 503 *Lord President*, having brought in an express from the North, backs off to its home shed at Haymarket in about 1947. Gresley V1 No 7659 on shunting duties has probably drawn out the incoming stock and so released No 503. The A2/2 although quite a good-looking machine, lacks the grandeur of the P2s and especially the original No 2001 *Cock O The North*.

Opposite: The splendid original Gresley streamlined designs as 2-8-2 Class P2 were rebuilt under the stewardship of Thompson as 4-6-2s into Class A2/2. Treated to this during the time of the D-Day landings *Earl Marischal* went back into traffic in June 1944. The originally numbered No 2003 *Lord President* was dealt with at the same time and returned to service from Doncaster in December 1944, and was a drab looking machine in early 1946 before a repaint and being renumbered in June 1946 as No 503 as seen on the previous page.

Top Right: Allocated to Gateshead in July 1947, the locomotive *Great Northern* now in LNER green livery and numbered 113, was observed at Berwick hauling the up "Flying Scotsman". Test runs were arrange to compare the performance of No 113 and A4 No 31 *Golden Plover* between Edinburgh and Dundee; seen here on the outskirts of Edinburgh. *Great Northern* was transferred to Haymarket depot on 2 September 1947. During her sojourn in Scotland the locomotive completed 862 miles, 626 of which were on these test trips. Details of the runs are contained in the RCTS Book 2A on LNER Locomotives. No 113 returned South on 12 September 1947.

Bottom Right: Great Northern on the 2pm ex Waverley express for Dundee and Aberdeen running with steam sanders going, alongside the 2pm to Glasgow Queen Street. The Glasgow passengers are showing real interest. The race would be truly joined on leaving Haymarket station over the two or three miles of parallel lines before diverging to the north and west. It was not unknown for the lads of Haymarket shed to place bets as to which of their engines would pass the depot first.

Above: Leuchars Junction in Fife was the mainline station to change at for St Andrews. Besides the expresses and local passenger traffic through the station, coal from the numerous mines in the shire meant there was a steady stream of trains trundling empty and full wagons at regular intervals. A typical scene shows LNER J38 No 1424 returning empties from the north in the summer of 1938.

Below: Although it is often quoted that the LNER V2s were the engines that won the war, one such example No 4778 captured by my camera in 1938 draws in to stop a full year before hostilities, although matters in Spain had already raised concerns for the peace. All up and down passenger trains except "The Aberdonian" stopped at Leuchars Junction. Through sleeping cars on "The Night Scotsman", met the needs of passengers wishing to change to or from St Andrews at this point. The road vehicles are a delightful addition to this period view.

Below: Montrose, forty miles south of Aberdeen was also a splendid place to stop off with a camera. LNER A1 No 2563 *William Whitelaw* drifts in on an Aberdeen-Edinburgh Express. Behind the tender is a fish van followed by a 1400 gallon glass lined road/rail tanker with milk for Bradford. It had been brought into Aberdeen from a centre in the country by road. The LMS carriages in the bay platform were used to connect Montrose passengers with the LMS main line at Bridge of Dun.

Above: Montrose with Inverbervie Branch included on the station name board. The bay platform was shared with this branch (under LNER control) and the LMS service to Brechin. Ex CR coaches are at present occupying the platform. This up train, obviously consisting of mainline stock, is probably, a mid morning express from Aberdeen. Usually this would either be rostered for an A1, A3 or even a P2. Were the unidentified ex NBR Locos now classified J37 and D29 on duty as a result of an engine failure further north?

Above: The relief roads were to the west of the station beside a large tidal estuary. LNER D49 No 266 *Forfarshire* draws in, with a light northbound goods. The height of the bridge in the background over the sea inlet gives some indication of the steep rising gradient from the station. This climb continues in all at 1 in 80 and 1 in 110 for 3.5 miles to Usan before the dip to Lunan Bay. In addition to some severe curves, the line was single track and therefore required token exchanges. It was the only part of the East Coast Mainline so restricted and a real test of a driver's skill with a 500-ton train, as the up "Aberdonian" usually was.

Fresh Fish for London

Right: Waverley station was suffused with the fresh odour of fish and the seaside when the 1.45pm ex Aberdeen No 1 express fish train for Kings Cross stopped to change engines. These daily trains were exceptionally heavy workings as attested by the presence of P2 No 2005 *Thane of Fife* on the incoming train in 1937. This evocative name was one of four selected for the class from a competition of the day in Boys Own Paper magazine. The Thane is the name of the Lord of the old Scottish Kingdom of Fife.

Opposite: Depending on the season, more than one train would run. In 1951 the same train was caught approaching Longniddry, appropriately enough hauled by Thompson's A2/3 No 60524 *Herringbone.* The name derived from Lord Derby's magnificent racehorse of the same name that won both the 1000 Guineas and the St. Leger in 1943. The name was awarded to the locomotive from entering traffic new in September 1947. She lasted just eighteen years in service, before finishing up discarded to the Motherwell Machinery & Scrap Company's yards for breaking in May 1965. Oh what a waste!

Top Right: Even a distinguished A4 was not excused from taking a turn to get supplies to Billingsgate Market. As witnessed by 60016 *Silver King* getting to grips with its task passing Aberlady Junction during 1954. This up service was privileged to pass through Waverley station. Normally goods traffic was diverted in both directions onto the southern arc of the suburban line, so avoiding the main station. Empty vans returning from Kings Cross to Aberdeen used this route.

Below: Stanier 2-8-0 8Fs were not a common sight in Scotland. This unidentified locomotive, taken on the through road at Portobello, looks as if it had been put on the Aberdeen fish express between Edinburgh and Newcastle. None the less she seems to be making good progress with this important train.

Aberdeen Awa'

Above: The joint station in Aberdeen was not only the end of the line for traffic from Euston, Kings Cross, Edinburgh and Glasgow, but also from Inverness, the fishing ports and holiday resorts of the North East and Deeside. As a consequence, a remarkable mixture of locomotives came and went. Indeed for variety it could rival Carlisle, although its disadvantage lay in the fact that it was so remote. Pre-war, the LNER was represented by P2s, V2s, A1s, A3s, an occasional A4, a number of former NBR and GNSR locomotives as well as ex GER B12s. When the fate of the P2s hung in the balance, LNER W1 No 10000 appeared on a round test trip from Edinburgh. The LMS turned up an occasional Princess and streamlined Pacific, also a regular display of Royal Scots, Jubilees, Black Fives, Compounds and Moguls. For an exhibition of locomotives and rolling stock held on 14 and 15 November 1936, 4-6-2 Turbomotive No 6202 was sent to the Granite City. Streamlined No 6229 *Duchess of Hamilton* was observed in service, turned out in grey with white stripes; presumably before being finally painted for "The Coronation Scot" visit to the USA in 1939. Gresley P2 No 2002 *Earl Marischal* waits with a fish van to join its train for the South. Note the ex East Coast Joint coach at the adjacent platform. The date was August 1939, and the platform edges and roof supports were lined in white in anticipation of the blackout to come.

Above: Happier days in 1937. A pristine London North Eastern Railway V2 No 4787 ready to depart on the 3.45pm express for Edinburgh. Just above the tender, a signal shows 'off' for the departing 3.30pm London Midland & Scottish Railway's train to Glasgow Buchanan Street.

Above: A grubby London Midland & Scottish Railway Jubilee No 5723 *Defiance* and an unidentified but highly polished compound on down trains in 1938. No gentleman would be seen without his hat, when out and about in the Thirties. The gabardine raincoat would be a necessity with the vagaries of Aberdeenshire weather.

Opposite: Not far from the shed, LMS 4P5F Mogul No 2809 rolls past Ferryhill signal box, backing down for duty. In the distance is ex GER B12 No 8548 awaiting signal clearance. Twenty-five of these exiled B12's worked at one time or another in the area usually to the North East coast or Deeside lines. In the summer, they found favour for excursion and tourist use and fifty members of the class were also temporarily allocated elsewhere in Scotland.

Above: The elegance of this ex North British Railway D31 No 9729 has to be admired while she percolates gently in the storage sidings near Ferryhill. Sadly few of her type would make it to Nationalisation and the British Railways era after the war. We are left with this reminder of these fine machines with this 1938 view, before the horrors to come the following year.

Right: One of the two ex Great North of Scotland Railway purchases of this design from Manning Wardle in 1915. Specifically taken on to work at Aberdeen's quayside, where they stayed all their working lives, aside from the odd works trip to Inverurie for works attention. Now in the guise as LNER Class Z4 No 6844, a compact and sturdy 0-4-2T built to negotiate the sharp radii curves encountered in and around these busy docks, as seen here in 1939. The first of the pair to be withdrawn was in March 1959 and the second was withdrawn and replaced by diesels in April of the following year.

Above: Perhaps beauty and the beast are seen together as LMS Royal Scot No 6125 *3rd Carabinier* awaits to depart at 3.30pm on the up West Coast Postal. Another ex GNSR locomotive now classified as LNER Class D40 No 6846 *Benachie* is leaving on the 3.20pm stopping train to Ballater. Just visible at the right of the picture, can be seen a small part of the road/rail milk tank carrying produce from Kittybrewster to Bradford via York on the 3.45pm Edinburgh Express. The safety lining for blackout purposes is evident on the platform edges. The photograph was taken at the end of August 1939, less than a week before the outbreak of war. Photography of transport subjects was forbidden from 3 September 1939 under emergency orders. This is one of my last railway photographs to be taken for 'the duration'. I now hand over to Dugald to take our story on to the end of steam.

Opposite: We begin at Glasgow Central in 1965, with a most appropriate reporting number being carried, the 'Caley 123' being engaged on an Easter special arranged by the Stephenson Locomotive Society. This was her last year of active service, before being set aside and later displayed in the Glasgow Museum of Transport.

Days and Nights at Glasgow Central

Left: Several types of 2-6-4 tanks could be found in control of empty carriage duties during this period. In this case the young and perhaps inexperienced although relaxed crew of this Fairburn designed engine 42199, keep an eye on activities at the adjacent platforms during this lay over at the terminus.

Opposite: A charming scene at the platform ends once again. This time the Riddles design of Standard 2-6-4 tank 80116 is on duty. The coaching stock is more modern, but we suspect that will be of little concern to the small child making his way along the platform. The locomotive crew, are not to be seen this time, but the porter is questioning the engine spotters checking their notes on the luggage trolleys. The coach dates this shot as being most likely as 1967 and the last few weeks of activity for this locomotive.

Left: Another of these Fairburn tanks from Polmadie, around the same time as the new blue and grey corporate image was being introduced, in particular along the West Coast Main Line. This time we are in the more experienced hands of the driver and guard at least. The fireman in earlier days would have spent a number of years as a cleaner before being allowed out of the shed precincts for firing turns on even empty stock duties. This locomotive worked the last rostered steam passenger train on the Scottish Region on Friday, 28 April, 1967.

Opposite: A mid afternoon departure for Gourock from Glasgow Central is taking on further passengers, and back in the less frantic sixties there was always time for a blather with the engine crew. In this case our Standard Five is still proudly wearing her Corkerhill shedplate. She was the last of a batch of just five engines ordered in the 1954 programme for the Scottish Region. These were built at Derby Works during April and May 1955, but eleven years later the end is nigh.

Opposite: With little work for a while until the train engine takes back out the stock that one of Polmadie's Standard Fives has brought in, all is quiet aside from the sounds of steam gently emitting and the station announcers voice echoing around the station. Hopefully the fireman has a low fire and has filled the boiler as they arrived, it would certainly not do for her to blow her safety valves at 225 lb.sq.in at the buffer stops.

Above: In the presence of one of the shiny "Blue Trains" in the adjoining platform. One of Leeds Holbeck's last serviceable Jubilees 45593 *Kolhapur* has brought in a Summer extra, most likely from Scarborough. The weather forecast can not have been too favourable before the journey, as the ladies have taken the precaution of bringing their coats. Much of this traffic was to disappear in the following decade, as resorts in Spain, would become more attractive to holidaymakers from Glasgow.

Opposite: The only Britannia unfortunate enough not to bare a name was 70047 seen here, about to step out herself into the heavy rainfall with an excursion back to the south. The engine has a good head of steam and will be well up to task by the looks of things, even if slippery rails are encountered getting away. Many worthy names have been put forward over the years, in keeping with the principles of the class as to what this engine could have been named including Florence Nightingale, Charles Darwin and even The Boys Brigade.

Right: This driver has perhaps stepped out into the better light of the station from his cab to read his weekly notices, while he awaits the release of his locomotive Britannia 70033 *(Charles Dickens)*. The ever present porters' trolleys of Glasgow Central also wait their next turns of duty. The width of the platforms shows well in this view to anticipate for the expected heavy traffic when the station was being built in Victorian times.

Above: The last year of Duchess operation for the terminus started in January 1964 with a number of trains being diverted as Euston was being rebuilt and the famous Doric Arch being dismantled in an act of official vandalism. This cold evening found 46254 *City of Stoke on Trent* preparing to leave on the 7pm to Euston diverted to Marylebone. This engine had in fact just come back out of storage because of the shortage of motive power at Crewe North. She would gain more months in the service of the railway until September of that year and was quickly cut up by Christmas of 1964 by Cashmore's of Great Bridge.

Below: Several weeks later saw another Duchess standing in for the rostered English Electric Type Four in the shape of 46225 *Duchess of Gloucester* on this same service. Driver Taylor of Crewe North was eagerly anticipating a good run and expected to catch the 'Postal' which was away before him. His mate would have a real job before him satisfying the Pacific's needs climbing Craigenhill, Beattock and Shap. As well as assisting his driver to sight signals including those lit only with oil lamps against a dark and misty night with drifting steam, in the harsh conditions of a steam footplate. Romantic, yes but very skilled and nerve racking at times.

Left: The Home Internationals Scotland versus England football specials for their return in April 1964 was to be in the hands of Duchesses. Here Driver Birtles of Crewe North stands alongside 46251 *City of Nottingham*, while more mailbags are loaded on board behind him. The engine's headlamps are well trimmed and shining bright as they should be, and the then favoured train reporting number is affixed to the smokebox.

Opposite: With a similar reporting number stands 46256 *Sir William Stanier FRS* with another train on this evening. It will be noticed that the headlamps do not seem to shine as bright, and one hopes that the fireman has yet to attend to this, if only to protect his train while it stands awaiting departure. Just like *City of Stoke on Trent* this engine would find its way to Great Bridge in time for Christmas and certainly not be available for service in 1965!

66A Polmadie - By Day and Night

Opposite: Drifting easily past the depot with a short rake of parcels vans in the winter of 1965 was Class 6P5F Pacific 72009 *Clan Stewart*. This engine was the last built in her class for Scotland when delivered in March 1953. The intended further five for the Southern Region and another ten for Scotland were cancelled, although the authorities even managed to get around to working out what the names should be. It really was strange that that last Britannia was not named after all.

Right: Wearing what is really an incorrect shedplate painted on for 50E Scarborough whose depot closed in 1963 is Standard 9F 2-10-0 92231. With a satisfying glow from the firebox doors into her cab and the pull of the home signal she has the off in 1966, after being serviced at the shed for her next duty back south of the border.

Left: Both the rays from a sunny lunchtime and the gas lamps within the shed help to illuminate the work weary flanks of Britannia 70036 *(Boadicea)* in 1965. By this stage the nameplates had been removed from just about all of the class, as witnessed here. Some were to benefit from hand painted replicas to restore some dignity.

Opposite: Appearing only slightly cleaner on a much colder and duller day outside the shed by the inspection pits we find the same locomotive, ready for departure from the depot. As can be seen by the figure trudging his way across the tracks it was definitely a day for being well wrapped up.

Left: Along the other side of the Britannia was one of many Standard Class 4 tanks often to be found at the depot. The atmospheric nature of steam lends itself more readily perhaps to mood photography than the more modern forms of traction, which replaced it.

Right: Many opportunities arose to capture the railway scene as exemplified here by two colleagues discussing the order of work in front of another pair of Britannia Pacifics. Thanks to the late Willie Sharp BR Scottish Region for the provision of photographic permits as on this visit to the shed in 1965.

Left: The fireman has just replaced the lamp on the tender of his Britannia 70039 *(Sir Christopher Wren).* While a guard walking towards the camera carries his own shiny handlamp and a can of lamp oil to recharge the lamps he required on his brake van. The oil would also be good for helping to start the fire in the stove of a freezing cold brake van.

Opposite: This Black Five has been stopped for attention to the front tube plate by a fitter, who has come prepared as can be seen by the presence of the portable oxyacetylene gear to the right. The puddles catching the light in the shed would most likely have been from boiler washouts, and the fact the fitter would require the boiler empty of water.

Opposite: Most visitors to Polmadie around 1965 will recall seeing the 'foreign' Pacifics stabled at the back of the shed. In late 1963 three Thompson A2/3s and three Peppercorn A2s were transferred here supposedly to replace the Duchesses. An unpopular move, though it presumably made sense to the beancounters. "They NB engines" did do some secondary passenger and parcels work but were laid up and withdrawn within two years. Only A2 60530 *Sayajirao* escaped to Dundee for use there.

Right: The differences in the front ends of Peppercorn 60535 *Hornets Beauty* and Thompson's A2/3 60512 *Steady Aim* are readily apparent in this view. Perhaps as her name suggests, the Peppercorn engine appeared to be more elegant to some eyes. If officialdom had retained the Duchesses, they certainly would have seen more work, or was that the game of politics being played?

Opposite: Another great Stanier design appreciated by all engine men was his Black Five. Sent to Newton Heath depot in Manchester when new in 1935, this example 45106 had now passed to 12A Carlisle Kingmoor. Once watered by her crew she would get away off shed to work a train back, most likely to the Border City once more. One of the short-lived Clayton Type One diesels lurks in the darkness as an ominous threat to the survival of steam.

Right: Further up in the yard was the 'grid' provided by the LMS to make the task of fire dropping an easier and safer one. On this evening a Britannia has worked to the depot for disposal, and hopefully the fireman has kept a very light fire on board 70054 (*Dornoch Firth*). This was the last built of her class and formerly carried the most northerly name of the six Scottish Firths chosen as names for these Pacifics.

Opposite: Stabled in the cover of the shed on a damp Glasgow evening are two more Britannias in light steam awaiting their next turns. Both engines have the modified smoke deflectors favoured by the Western Region after their bad experiences with the class and sighting signals. Based at Kingmoor from October 1964, 70016 (*Ariel*) managed almost another three years working from Carlisle, often visiting Glasgow. After her withdrawal and a couple of months in store at her last home, she was to join twenty one of her classmates to be scrapped at McWilliams Yard at Shettleston in the south eastern suburbs of Glasgow and former North British territory.

Right: Just to show that some of the Thompson A2/3s did manage some work, 60522 *Straight Deal* is seen in the company of another of those Clayton Type One diesels which would become a brief feature of the depot, and a much more respected Standard Class 5 73059. The name of *Straight Deal* does not refer to a card game in an engineman's bothy nor to successive goverments' treatment of the railways, but to the winning horse of the 1943 Derby at Epsom.

Left: Also making an interesting pattern with escaping steam in the cold night air on the depot was 72008 *Clan Macleod* visiting from Kingmoor. This Pacific was released from Crewe Works in February 1952 and was the second longest-lived of her class surviving for a mere fourteen years and two months. Only 72006 *Clan Mackenzie* survived longer being withdrawn in the following month May 1966. The Clans were split between both Kingmoor and Polmadie for their working lives, with only the occasional special working taking them away from their regular duties.

Opposite: On another of my regular evening calls at the depot armed with both camera and tripod Britannia 70016 *(Ariel)* was found by the driver's inspection and oiling up pits. The motive power of the future is also on shed in the form of a Brush Type Four diesel. As mentioned earlier a number of Britannia's although not allocated to Scottish sheds found their way to Scottish scrapyards, with a grand total of forty five of the fifty five strong class being purchased by the countries scrap dealers.

Left: With nameplates still attached is the poet *John Milton* whose name has been taken by Britannia 70005. Again the smoke deflectors have been modified to remove the handrails and replace them in this case with round rather than the oval handholds. Another of the ever present Clayton Type One diesels can be seen and behind the Pacific is one of the Standard Class 3 Moguls. Night-time photography would often benefit from the reflected light after a rain shower such as on this evening.

Glasgow Queen Street

Opposite: One of the Thompson B1s 61191 from 64A St.Margarets has arrived at the terminus with a summer extra in 1964. The shine on the smokebox door suggests that it has been repainted after a little hard work for the locomotive has scorched the old paint away.

Opposite: Another summer extra this time from Scarborough has brought in Gresley V2 60813 carrying the unique smoke deflectors and plain stove pipe style of chimney. The three ticket collectors by the barrier will be a match for the party of school children and the lady with the very blonde hair approaching behind them.

Right: A more conventional chimney is fitted to another V2 also with the original inside steam pipes which has arrived with another of these popular summer extras of the period from Scarborough. One of the station's cleaning ladies is already making her way to help sweep out the stock for its next duty.

Opposite: Photographing the cameramen and spotters for the visit of Peppercorn A2 60527 *Sun Chariot* as the motive power for this leg of the SLS Easter special of 1964 certainly enhances the picture.

Above: Perhaps the last Gresley A3 to visit Queen Street in regular service was 60052 *Prince Palatine* as one of the last two that survived at Edinburgh's St.Margarets shed? Once again having brought in a Scarborough to Glasgow extra in the summer of 1964.

Opposite: A pleasant surprise at Easter 1966 was the use of A4 60019 *Bittern* to work a special for Edinburgh. Perhaps another last visit in regular service and brought about after having had minor repairs at Cowlairs.

Below: Surely the last former North British locomotive to grace this former railways Glasgow terminus was *Glen Douglas*. The D34 4-4-0 arrived after running rather late on an enthusiasts' special in August 1965 into one of the old West Highland Line platforms.

Buchanan Street

Opposite: A rather bleak winters day across the city, with steam rising from not only a couple of Black Fives and an A4 but hopefully the steam heating of one of their successors, a Birmingham Railway & Carriage Works Type Two in 1965.

Right: The arrival on a warmer day when it was more comfortable for two generations of enthusiast to stop and admire Peppercorn A2 60528 *Tudor Minstrel*, which was one of the last three at Dundee Tay Bridge during 1966.

Opposite: It seems that even the driver cannot help himself but to get out and admire the lines of his Pacific, and take the admiration of his onlookers as the last of the passengers departs.

Right: The next arrival was *Sir Nigel Gresley* himself whose cylinder drain cocks are filling the concourse with steam as the trains' guard makes his way off shift. In the meantime a few more sacks of mail have arrived for onward movement.

In Pursuit of A4s

Opposite: Standing among the alighting passengers gave me this view as several ladies have come to town perhaps on an afternoons shopping expedition. To my right stands A4 *Lord Farringdon* having brought the train in from Aberdeen.

Right: Another of the Gresley A4s named after one of the LNER's Chief General Manager was 60006 *Sir Ralph Wedgwood* awaiting departure on the 5.30pm to Aberdeen. The lights of the signal oil lamps shine bright in this time exposure, certainly brighter than they would appear to the driver and his fireman through the smoke and steam on their footplate.

Left: With a superb plume of smoke to show the driver's intent on the pull away from Buchanan Street is A4 60007 *Sir Nigel Gresley*. The crews of the Standard Five and the Birmingham Railway Carriage & Wagon Type Two will have noted this departure into the dusk as well.

Opposite: Taken a few weeks later after the evenings had drawn in a little more in a shower of rain, the same locomotive is ready for the right away once more as the driver leans out awaiting the 5.30pm departure time for Aberdeen. Slippery rails this time would produce even more fireworks?

Above: The chasing of these departures became something of a ritual at the time for the enjoyment the photography could bring. Departure time is approaching and A4 60010 *Dominion of Canada* has the lead in this evening's show, with one of St.Rollox's Caprotti Standard Fives and Black Five 45423 as the supports at Buchanan Street.

Opposite: The Springbok badge on this side of 60009 *Union of South Africa* stands proud, as she waits her turn on these three hour expresses as I sought out the 5.30pm departure once more.

Opposite: As can be seen the flanks of 60009 *Union of South Africa* only bore the badge on the one side. This visit was on a cold and frosty night, when the engine crew would have felt the biting wind at 60mph plus on their journey north, while I was away back to my fireside after work.

Right: One of the regulars on this turn during this Indian Summer albeit lasting right through the dark winter nights, as the Gresley A4's on the Aberdeen trains brought out enthusiasts from all over the country to catch their last workings.

Opposite: This fireman has proably seen me at work before as he looks out of his cab, in the glow of the open firebox doors of 60010 *Dominion of Canada.*

Below: The menacing structures of high rise living, Glasgow's Red Road, flats another poor idea of the Sixties rise above St. Rollox or Balornock, as it was known in Caledonian days. On shed in the crisp and pleasing light are Black Five 45016, Standard Caprotti Five 73146 and the two A4s to enhance the scene, *Lord Faringdon* and *Sir Ralph Wedgwood.* As might be expected several more Black Fives were on shed that day as well.

Opposite: Passing St. Rollox shed is one of its own allocation of A4s 60031 *Golden Plover* with the 6.15pm Buchanan Street to Dundee service, while the A4 off the 1.30pm train from Aberdeen has just come on shed.

Right: On the footplate of 60019 *Bittern* as we reversed out of Aberdeen 'Joint' Station for Ferryhill, signs of the substantial fish traffic could be found in the sidings being shunted by one of Glasgow's less successful products from the North British Locomotive Company.

Left: The opening of the 'cod's mouth' arrangement to gain access to the smokebox for cleaning would often draw a crowd of onlookers. Quick-witted enginemen would kid on the more gullible that they were winding the engine up like a big clockwork toy. However one suspects that the trilby hatted yard foreman has heard and seen it all before at Aberdeen Ferryhill.

Opposite: With the lower flap also open now, the engine has been taken to the turntable for turning to make life a little easier in clearing out the ash from the smokebox with the winter wind of the North Sea coast in mind, not a bad idea. The chap on the right has a substantial pair of steel toe capped boots for the job, and the extended shovel and scraper are at hand already in the 'cod's mouth'.

Opposite: After coaling the next job at hand would be filling the tender with water outside the shed at Ferryhill. Both varieties of tender with and without corridor connections were found side by side on this visit. With 60024 *Kingfisher* on the left and 60019 *Bittern* on the right.

Right: Hidden to the right of Bittern was one of the five A2s rebuilt with double chimney and multiple valve regulator 60532 *Blue Peter*. Her driver is just starting his oiling round and is preparing his oilcan with a fresh charge from the stores.

Glasgow St.Enoch Station

Opposite: In the latter years a Duchess would be a regular leaving Glasgow at 5.30pm but from the Glasgow & South Western Railway terminus before my regular visits to the ex Caledonian Railway station to catch the A4s began. This departure at 5.30pm was the 'Parly' to Carlisle via the 'Sou-West'. In charge on this evening in 1964 was 46244 *King George VI.*

Above: The driver of another service has come across for a word while they both wait departure time on this damp misty night. Some idea of the visibility can be gained from this view, as these experienced men knew all their signals, strange noises at particular points on the track and bridges and landmarks to let them know where they were and if the road was clear at all times, not to mention their own nerves of steel and faith in the signalmen along their route.

Opposite: Making a thunderous exit from the station on this working is Duchess Pacific 46249 *City of Sheffield* as the setting sun's rays catch St.Enoch for the last time that day. The wonderful care in detail taken by some of the pre-grouping companies using their shareholders money can be seen as an investment so many years later when one enjoys the scrolls and intricacy of the lamp standards and the ornate ironwork over the great station roof.

Right: A year or so later and the Duchesses have all gone and a Britannia has charge of this service. Flanked to the left by the lights of the suburban coaches of a local headed by another Standard design, of a Class 4 tank engine, and even these are being superseded by the advance of diesel multiple units into their work. That ironwork really was a wonder to behold, lost when the station closed in 1966.

Opposite: Another of the Standard Class 4s waits for the starting signal, as a British Railways built 'Peak' diesel gets away first, with a Kilmacolm train on the line to Greenock Princes Pier; the use of this as motive power for this type of suburban service might be considered as unusual.

Below: Inside under that splendid overall roof I recorded Standard Class 4 80004 one of the regulars on East Kilbride trains. On which I regularly commuted in the sixties.

Meanwhile Over in the East

Opposite: Believe it or not this was taken on a summers day albeit very wet and misty at Edinburgh Waverley in 1965 as Gresley V2 was departing. The tower of the North British Hotel appears as if from the backscene of a Wagnerian Opera through the mist.

Right: The last A2 run from Edinburgh to Carlisle via the North British Waverley Route and back via the Caley brought me to the capital in October 1966. A memorable climb was made behind 60532 *Blue Peter* up Beattock. The previous week she had been scheduled to do a return trip from Glasgow to Carlisle, and had in fact been at the head of the train in Central Station when due to poor loading the special was cancelled. Those who had booked were given a complimentary trip to Carlisle with a visit around Kingmoor depot thrown in!

Opposite: The special made a stop at Hawick on the Waverley Route. In the foreground are two 'weel kent faces', second and third from left, W.A.C. Smith and the late James L. Stevenson both at the time British Railways Scottish Region staff, the latter its Planning Manager. How grateful we are to them and others such as the late Roy Hamilton and Stuart Sellar, who have recorded the railway scene so comprehensively.

Right: A similar debt of gratitude should be expressed to Alan Pegler who managed to preserve 4472 *Flying Scotsman* in 1963 and restore her to the mainline before some of the then new rulers of the railway sought to make it as difficult as possible. In 1968 she had just managed to make it non-stop into Edinburgh Waverley, completing the fortieth anniversary run of the 'Non - Stop' from Kings Cross.

Above: Having made it although very short of water, 4472 was uncoupled and went in search of replenishment. Even with the extra tender. It was a difficult run as some of the water troughs had been taken out, as they were no longer needed by the diesels running the service at the time. How satisfactory it is for this locomotive to have been secured for our splendid National Railway Museum at York.

Opposite: Another Gresley A3 at Edinburgh Waverley in the company of two Deltics to the right of the station, towards the end of that long line of cars. The precision and complexity of the trackwork allows the passage of 60083 *Sir Hugo* light engine past the station signal box to gain the platform to meet the waiting coaches of its train in 1964. Many observers will have trekked up the steps seen to my right to have gained this fine vantagepoint. Although today the trackwork is a lot simpler in its layout and regular steam and Deltic activity is long gone.

Left: In the early evening of a Saturday in February 1965, the return working of a rugby special to Aberdeen was waiting at Waverley, with A4 60004 *William Whitelaw* at the head. The A4 had gained the name of the Chairman of the LNER in 1941 after previously being called *Great Snipe*; the Chairman's name had been upgraded from its place on an A1 No 2563 before it was rebuilt as an A3 and renamed as *Tagalie.*

Opposite: The stirring name of *Bonnie Dundee* was awarded to Peppercorn's A1 60159, found hidden away inside the sheds at 64B Haymarket, along with a selection of B1s and V2s, together with one of the English Electric Type Fours that were to become a fixture of the depot for over twenty years. The depot officially closed to steam on 8 September 1963.

Above: The next Peppercorn A1 numerically, was 60160 *Auld Reekie*, one of Haymarket's number two link engines, seen towering over the former North British Railway J36 65243 *Maude*. Nowadays this old soldier is happily preserved by the Scottish Railway Preservation Society whose members have also so energetically fought to preserve our industrial and engineering heritage.

Opposite: Aah! That delicious and unmistakable aroma of the steam shed, even in its final days as the visitor stopped for a minute or two to enjoy the effect of steam and light upon *Hal O' the Wynd* visiting Haymarket from the Peppercorn A1s home shed of 52D Tweedmouth just to the south of Berwick-upon-Tweed. In the next road is A4 60024 *Kingfisher* who was on its home shed and transferred to 64A St.Margarets when Haymarket closed to steam.

Opposite: If you started on the railway with a career path set on becoming a driver you would have started with this view of a Pacific such as A1 60161 *North British*. Your first few years would have been spent drawing cotton waste and paraffin from the stores each day and cleaning the grime from the motion, frames, wheels and so on.

Above: The glory might come later on after you had become a passed cleaner, fireman, passed fireman and finally after much perseverance, dedication, possibly with a depot move or two, you would find yourself in one of the links as a driver. Then as here you might find the responsibility of the regulator of a fine Pacific, and the safety of the train yours.

Opposite: Regrettably I did not note the kind drivers name who gave me a 'hurl' on the A1 60155 *Borderer* from St.Margarets to Millerhill to take this goods southward, in the summer of 1964. I made one brave attempt with the shovel, and failed as *Borderer* hit a crossing and went sideways or so it seemed to me. What is more she was one of five of her class fitted with roller bearings and superb locomotives they were!

Right: Safely back at 64A St. Margarets within the long shed to enjoy the patterns the light and shade made upon the roofing timbers. Inside among the gathering diesels were A3 60052 *Prince Palatine* and an A4 among the less glamorous tank engines from Fairburn and Riddles in 1965.

Below: Out in the shed yard at St. Margarets I took this study of wheels. One of Edward Thompson's underrated Pacifics A2/3 60512 *Steady Aim* along with one of his best designs, a B1. Take a further look at the two designs of wheels to those delightful wheelbarrows, the older one to the right has gracefully curved spokes.

Opposite: If I might be forgiven in assuming this as the Prince and a Pauper. For the wages of St. Margarets firelighter could not have been much back in 1964. Nonetheless he keeps a keen eye on both me and A3 60052 *Prince Palatine* which is making steam to go off shed and take up her train later that night.

Opposite: Our Prince once more in daylight this time, getting away from Millerhill with the 6.15pm fitted goods to Craiginches Yard, Aberdeen in 1965. Were the A3's 6'8" driving wheels ideal for this type of work?

Above: Steam, and plenty of it! Again in 1965 the 6.15pm to Craiginches has a Pacific in charge with A4 60024 *Kingfisher,* while one of the English Electric Type Four's crew pops up through the bonnet hatch to clean the windows to the right.

Border City & Miscellany

Opposite: Sir Nigel and Sir William meet again on the last run of a Duchess in British Railways ownership. The Scottish Lowlander special run on 26 September 1964 had brought Duchess 46256 *Sir William Stanier FRS* from Crewe, and A4 60007 *Sir Nigel Gresley* would take the train onwards over the Waverley Route.

Right: The time honoured innocent pleasure of train-spotting, wear your anorak with pride! About to head North in 1966 was Britannia 70014 (*Iron Duke*), now coupled to one of the later type of BR1D tenders with increased coal and water capacity which it has gained from a withdrawn class mate, possibly 70052 *Dornoch Firth*?

Below: While others were engaged in other matters on Boxing Day 1967, I slipped off to photograph Britannia 70013 *Oliver Cromwell* at a time when all of the remaining Pacifics, all Britannia's were being withdrawn. Even the signalman has come to his window to watch the spectacle.

Opposite: Rostered to work this football special away from Carlisle, and the demise of steam imminent, I could not resist the going away shot against this lovely cloud scape. The locomotive was working hard and lifted the post Christmas spirits no end.

Below: So much so another shot was called for as a Sulzer Type Two came the other way running light engine. The family group out for a walk along the riverbank also stopped a while to enjoy the passing of steam that day too, although the lady with the bag seems unconcerned.

Opposite: Further evidence of rationalisation of our railways was everywhere, such as here on St. Rollox High Bank as a British Railways Standard 9F lifts a very heavy oil train past the signal box a year earlier.

Left: Rebuilt Patriot 45531 *Sir Frederick Harrison* leaves Kennishead on the last lap of a Carlisle local up the 'Sou-West' to Glasgow St.Enoch in 1965. The home is off for a train coming the other way while I concentrate on the sulpherous exhaust of this Ivatt rebuild of the original Fowler design of 1930.

Right: That old favourite of the East Kilbride services, Standard Class 4 tank 80004 slows for the driver to pick up the tablet for the single line from Busby in 1965. Although the windows to the signal box locking room were most likely bricked up as a wartime measure, thankfully the thoughtful lamp and equally graceful design of lattice post signal remained from Caledonian Railway days, albeit with later LMS upper quadrant arms.

Left: Another exchange with moving trains but this time at speed, was the pick up of Royal Mail. One of the last pick-ups in use was near Larbert. The postman has already locked the hut where the spare leather pouches were kept for this operation, and remains to supervise the safe pick up. This type of operation would certainly save on time and help speed the delivery of mail to its destination, but would not have been too kind to any small delicate parcels perhaps.

Opposite: The rudimentary but useful hut for the well being of locomotive crews and their convenience provided at Gourock was looking a little worse for wear towards the end of steam operation on this line. The windows would have been welcomed by the enginemen to afford some protection from the wind and rain coming up the Clyde Estuary. The fireman of Standard Five 73079 leans out to ensure a clear road as they back off the turntable towards the station and the paddle steamer "Caledonia" moored in the background.

Opposite: Barking away under the cats cradle of catenary for the Blue Trains at Gourock is Black Five 45261, making its way with a rake of suburban coaches back up the Clyde towards Glasgow, again in 1965.

Right: What a day we had on "The Granite City" excursion. Part of this marathon tour to Aberdeen was double headed with John Cameron's privately owned A4 60009 *Union of South Africa* just out of sight behind a well turned out Black Five 44997. The train consisted of nineteen coaches, on the leg down to Perth from Aberdeen, with some very spirited running by both engine crews for the entertainment of all concerned.

Left: Back to Kennishead for a former LNER locomotive departure on one of the Carlisle locals in 1965. The steam thoughtfully picks out the outline of the smoke deflectors as Thompson A2/3 60522 *Straight Deal* gets away quickly in the cold air.

Opposite: Belying the great power of these Peppercorn A2s is 60530 *Sayajirao* quietly simmering inside the shed at St.Margarets. She may be dirty but her thoroughbred lines still show through the grime.

Left: I could hear *Sayajirao* climbing before she came around the corner through the rock cuttings on the climb up to the Forth Bridge with this Saturday van train for London from Dundee in 1965.

Opposite: One of Arthur Peppercorn's finest, A2 Pacific 60532 *Blue Peter* in her last few months of regular service in 1966, leaving Stirling for Glasgow on the 1.30pm from Aberdeen. Thankfully she was saved by the late Geoff Drury and was restored to mainline condition by the NELPG.

Above: The flags are out to assist in the Sunday wrong line working during an engineering occupation of Beattock Bank. The driver of the Fairburn Tank 42274 moves away under caution as his passengers look out to see what the delay is all about at Greskine. The signalman and his inspector seem to have it all under control in March 1967.

JOHN THOMAS 1914 – 1982

John belonged to Glasgow and possessed in abundance, the characteristic warm-hearted friendliness, down to earth common sense and good humour, lightly seasoned by the delightful eccentricity of that great City.

Of sturdy build, average height, partly bald and of fresh complexion, he was usually seen wearing a dark blue raincoat, a somewhat weathered felt hat and often with a camera slung over his shoulder. Apart from the camera he was, from all outward appearances, the ordinary chap in Sauchiehall Street. Once when attending hospital, the receptionist on taking his personal details, enquired as to his occupation. The poor girl's face was a study when, simply stating the fact, he answered 'author'.

Always ready for a chat by the wayside – on one occasion, a chat lasted for an hour and three-quarters! It seemed to pass in minutes for his conversation was beautifully phrased in a rather old fashioned style and delivered in a broad, rich, homely unaffected Scottish accent. A casual meeting was indeed a treat. There was no gossip, rather he would enthusiastically tell of a newly discovered fact, of an excursion or a club meeting recently enjoyed.

Once we met with no particular plan in view. John decided to show me around Springburn, the district that he named 'The Scottish Railway Metropolis'. It was fortunate that the traffic was light for we stopped frequently and comments and the history of local features followed.

John remembered how, just after noon the streets used to be filled by men hurrying home for dinner. Less than an hour later the flow was reversed, soon followed by the sound of the work's hooter. Then all was silent as it was on our excursion. And so it remains, for the railway works are no more.

Born in Springburn, he was the only son of John and Jeanne Thomas. His father was a moulder in the nearby railway works. Apart from wartime army service, he lived in the same tenement, high above the famous Cowlairs incline, for all of his life. Few railway movements took place, which he could not identify, from his eyrie. Indeed he probably knew the time of day by the events on the line below, without the looking at a clock.

Despite his warm friendly nature, oddly enough few were invited to visit his small flat in Gourlay Street. Perhaps a disguised shyness was the reason or that he felt it was not grand enough for entertaining. However, his home was beautifully refurbished and adequately although rather sparsely furnished. No television set for John. He appreciated the arts at first hand, however he allowed himself a radio for carefully selected programmes. Occasionally we attended the Scottish Opera together. Wagner's 'Meistersingers' is the performance I remember most of all. There we sat enthralled with the performance. Then during the long interval, enjoyed our sandwiches, downing them with a fizzy drink, as alcohol was not really to his taste. High up in the Theatre Royal, Glasgow, we couldn't have had a grander time at Glyndebourne.

He showed little regard for material possessions, but was content with his lot, searching through old records, writing, travelling and lecturing. He travelled to the USA and vastly enjoyed being introduced to their railways.

John was a bachelor. His old friend David L Smith married rather late in life. Margaret, David's delightful wife, always full of fun, once teased John about 'being next'. Poor John caught quite off guard, shuffled uncomfortably, stammered and blushed slightly. For once I saw a Glaswegian lost for words. I believe there was a special lady once a upon a time.

His religious beliefs were never paraded, if indeed he had any. He was kind and courteous. His modesty made him seem secretive; nevertheless his achievements gave him real satisfaction. An event that pleased him greatly was the literary lunch given by his then publishing house of David and Charles. Few authors have been more appropriately honoured – the meal was served in a dining car standing in his local station – Springburn.

In 1975 on the Stockton and Darlington anniversary, the BBC (an organisation he regarded with suspicion –"Bill you should always see the colour of their money first") invited him to take part in 'The Book Programme' representing railway authors. A fitting tribute to a senior member of the craft.

Much sought after as a speaker, his lectures were carefully planned and appropriate slides chosen, no matter the place or the status of the audience. His social highlights were railway excursions, exhibitions and club meetings. Tenacious in his views he was sensitive to criticism which was either met which stoney silence or a pokey jest.

He inaugurated and for a few years ran, a summer course at St. Andrews University on railway transport with excursions all over Scotland. He was in his element, unfolding the Scottish scene and telling tales of long ago, when locomotives steamed and simmered under their polished liveries of blue and green – and whatever colour it was that the NBR painted their engines. It was more like a club than an academic course. It was always over-subscribed, members coming from all over the country and from abroad. Great care was devoted to the timetable – it had to be. Marshalling a day trip from St. Andrews to Wick and back was no small undertaking – lasting 20 hours. 'Vicienti' was the first word on the postcard I received a few days later, franked Wick.

From an early age, it became apparent he was a born storyteller and writer. His articles, brief at first, appeared in boys' magazines and in the local press. After his death, a forty thousand-word manuscript was discovered entitled 'Life in a Glasgow School'.

Commenced in a youthful hand, the calligraphy became more adult as the work progressed. Photographs of the staff and pupils were added latterly, revealing his growing skill with a camera.

Some time after leaving school he became an insurance agent by day and an author by night. 'Obstruction, Danger' was his first published book in 1937. Later in life he did not find it to his satisfaction. The style was there, it only required refining to bring it up to the excellence one knows so well. Nevertheless it was favourably reviewed in the national press at Christmas for "the interested young man". 'Earthquakes in England' followed in 1938.

Called up in 1939 he was sent for training with the Highland Light Infantry in Maryhill Barracks, Glasgow. The railway-training centre at Longmoor, an army unit, recruited only from professional railwaymen. Mysteriously he got himself posted to the unit, to the displeasure of the commanding officer. As he put it, the war gave him a once in a lifetime chance to explore his hobby to the full. Private Thomas trained as a signalman. En route to India, the writing continued for the ship's magazine and later for the Forces press, while serving on the Bengal and Assam Railway. A small paperback on the Darjeeling and Himalaya Railway was completed and published in India; a railway he held in great affection. Later Corporal Thomas was called upon to write the official army account of the military control of the Bengal and Assam Railway. Back home he was allowed, with modifications to the text, to find a publisher and so, illustrated by his own superb photographs, the story reached the public.

Books on a wide variety of subjects followed – on Lawrence of Arabia, the Crusades, the Stephensons and Leonardo Da Vinci among others. Some were translated into German, Italian and Portuguese. When asked "why a book on Da Vinci?" His answer was simple. "Because I was asked to". A fortunate request as it went on to sell 27,000 copies in Italy alone.

Besides railways he had a great love of shipping, but for some reason he wrote little on the subject. Like his fellow citizens, a sail down the Clyde on a pleasure steamer was a real treat and a tonic to be savoured.

The acceptance by the fledgling house of David & Charles of his eleventh book 'The Springburn Story', marked a milestone in his career and one might hazard, also for the publishing house. The link was formed and from Devon came his Scottish railway masterpieces, 'The North British Railway', 'The NBR Atlantics', 'The Tay Bridge Disaster' and other volumes.

The West Highland Railway, probably his best and certainly most successful book, makes a splendid read even for someone without a particular interest in railways. John often took a day trip up this line, just for pleasure. Once he shared a compartment with a young American student. They were soon in conversation and the young lady to John's amusement, pointed out the features of the line in an instructing manner. After some time she drew from her haversack John's West Highland book, recommending it highly to the unsuspected author. A trip both would never forget!

His favourite work was 'The Callander and Oban Railway'. To begin with, 30,000 letters regarding the line's construction had to be consulted. Other histories on forgotten railways and regional histories gave him much pleasure in seeking out the peculiarities of smaller lines and their curious running practices.

He advised David and Charles regarding manuscripts on railway matters that had been submitted and edited the work of less experienced writers, so they would find their names gracing the title page of a book. John wrote as an historian. After scrutiny of original documents, which had often lain undisturbed since first deposited in the record offices, his attributes as a storyteller created a text that was unmistakable in style. The narrative flowed naturally and by the perfect choice of words, his descriptions were vivid, unhindered by unnecessary details, but enlivened with tales of people connected with the events described.

He had made a substantial start on writing the last volume of David and Charles' Railway Regional History of Great Britain series. Alas his health was deteriorating and the work had to pass to others to finish.

Projected when he died, was the history of "The LNER in Scotland" and some suitable photographs had been chosen. "The LMS History" was to be next.

He died in 1982. A room was named in his memory in his local library for apart from the Mitchell Library in Glasgow, it was his second home. One's lasting memory is of a courteous, unassuming, kind, fine Scotsman with a ready wit and an enormous literary ability.

John was indeed a true citizen of Glasgow and of his beloved Scottish Railway Metropolis.

Bill Rhind Brown, October 2004